THE SOLO SEX
JOKE BOOK

Jokes, Cartoons, and Limericks About the World's Most Popular Sex Act

Compiled by Ralph Mead, Ph.D

Cartoons by Christian Snyder

FACTOR PRESS
Post Office Box 8888
Mobile, Alabama 36689

ISBN 1-887650-17-2

DR. RALPH MEAD (a pseudonym) has taught psychology at several colleges and universities in the United States. He is also a counseling psychologist and consultant to schools and industries. For many years, he has been interested in all forms of humor and has found jokes about solo sex especially popular among the population in general and among males of all ages in particular. He hopes that this collection will not only titillate readers, but lead to a joyful acceptance of one of life's happiest and least expensive pleasures.

———————

CHRISTIAN SNYDER is currently "serving time" in New York State. Since his incarceration he has launched a career as a freelance magazine cartoonist, and has been published in both small and mainstream publications. He has also had his cartoons exhibited in art shows and his work has appeared on the World Wide Web. There's only one thing Christian enjoys doing *more* than drawing cartoons....

"Well Doc, isn't that the sickest sexual fantasy you ever heard in your life?"

CONTENTS

MASTURBATION AND HUMOR
Ralph Mead, Ph.D.

During the dozen or so years that I taught psychology at an all-men's college in the eastern United States, the topic of sex never failed to garner rapt attention from the young men sitting in those classrooms. When the topic came up, all eyes were glued on the podium. Students leaned forward slightly so that they would not miss a single word or nuance.

In a college classroom there is always a certain amount of rather subdued noise coming from students shuffling their feet, fidgeting in their chairs, turning pages in notebooks and displaying other minor signs of life. However, when my lectures got around to the topic of sex, there was always a sudden and marked reduction in the noise level, no matter how large the classroom. And when the discussion turned to masturbation, the total silence could be deafening. No other topic ever commanded such profound attention from these young men. Their ears were cocked and they strained to hear every word. Without exception, this reaction occurred every time I offered the course. Masturbation was a sure-fire topic, if there ever was one.

Calling attention to the students' sudden silence never failed to produce a wave of childish, somewhat nervous giggling all over the classroom. But when I punctuated the lecture with even the simplest joke about masturbation, the whole classroom exploded with boisterous laughter. Also, in every case, a few young men would wink at their seatmates or poke them in the ribs, strongly suggesting that the topic had some special, personal relevance to them.

The rather corny and hackneyed joke that I nearly always used went like this: I picked up a large sheaf of computer print-outs and, pretending to scrutinize them very carefully, announced, "I have here the poll results conducted just last month which showed that ninety-four percent of the men at this college admitted that they masturbated regularly and the other six percent were liars."

In those days, the joke was new!

Joking about masturbation seems to be universal among males. Men not only enjoy solo sex—they enjoy laughing about it as well. Why? We have all grown up being told by at least someone that jerking off is morally wrong—perhaps actually harmful in one fictitious way or another. Yet, each of us also knows that he has been personally and intimately involved in that very same "demeaning and possibly injurious" act. Conditions were such that we knew our buddies were also involved in this clandestine practice, mostly alone and in secret. In our youthful curiosity and in an attempt to understand ourselves in relation to our peers, we also talked about it, seriously exchanging myths and what few facts we had heard or read about this universal masculine pleasure.

Large numbers of naïve young males have been victimized by a prankster friend's "serious" revelation that very fine and almost invisible hairs grow in the palms of a masturbator's hands. And, upon discovering that they'd been duped, most of them couldn't wait to pull the same hoax on some of their other friends. Already at this stage in a young man's life, masturbation is not only fun but funny as well.

Later, in high school and college, masturbation is a topic of frequent and spirited discussion at bull sessions in the locker room, camping trips, and men's dormitories and fraternities. I recall one such session in which a young man reported that he had read a study which strongly indicated that masturbation was much more prominent among the highly educated. One of the other students in attendance at this informal seminar quickly blurted out, "Well, I guess this dorm is probably the best educated bunch of guys on campus." Another shouted, "I know some of you guys ought to breeze right through to a Ph.D."

On another occasion, when one of the men was preparing to show a pornographic film, his classmate produced a box of Kleenex and started passing it around the room. More peals of laughter and loud guffaws.

In my memory, a student rarely got caught jacking off in that dorm, but the keen interest in the topic left a clear impression that all of us practiced this solitary act and probably did so with considerable gusto. There was always the privacy of one's own room, where it could be accomplished discretely. In addition, if a man went to the shower room and found it empty, the temptation to beat off grew irresistible—especially when he got around to soaping up his genitals. (It should surprise no one that most men jack off in the shower.) Occasionally one of the men would comment that much more than soap and water went down the drain of that dorm's shower room.

Men who have been in the military also know that solo sex humor is used in ribald ways that all can

9

understand. If a man's bunk is a bit too squeaky, there was likely to be a jibe the next day that he was heard jacking off in the night. A frequent wake-up call in the barracks was the shout, "Get your hands off your cocks and onto your socks."

Another form of humor, limericks, have also focused on solo sex. These have been apprecited in the military as well. Consider the following, which is in general use in the navy and seems to have its origins in World War II:

'Twas off an Asian nation
We caused a great sensation.
A native junk
Was wrecked and sunk
By mutual masturbation.

Military men, college students, and others frequently joke with each other when they are doing their laundry or having it done for them. These jokes center around semen stains on bed sheets and underwear, direct results of jacking off, laughingly referred to as "pecker tracks."

Friends, talking together, occasionally punctuate the conversation with statements like "What's happened to all your usual energy? Been beating off too much?" When a man encounters a friend using a urinal or taking a leak along a wooded trail, he frequently will greet him by exclaiming, "If you shake it more than three times, you're playing with it!"

Similarly, and especially among young men, occasional contests arise in which the participants vie with each other concerning how far they can project their uninary streams. Such tournaments are especially likely to occur in a back street or alley on the way home after an evening of beer drinking. Contests like these also happen on camping trips when men feel the need to take a leak and stretch after sitting around a campfire.

These contests occasionally involve bodily discharges other than urine. Many men reveal that they, along with their good friends, have competed in masturbation bouts to determine who can shoot his semen the greatest distance. Perhaps less frequent, although quite common, are the contests in which men try to outdo each other in the number of times they can masturbate to orgasm in a given period of time—usually one 24-hour day. Almost always, participants follow an honor system so that each participant can enjoy privacy. Otherwise there would be ribald joking, laughter, and guffaws—which can easily deflate even the most persistent erection. The winner of these tournaments is treated with joking catcalls, and general merriment, and often a party attesting to his virility.

Some less admirable masturbational events frequently come about as a result of conspiratorial jokes. A prime example is the phony communal circle jerk session in which all but one member of the group is in on the deception. The proclaimed object of the contest is to determine who can reach climax and shoot his load in the shortest time. The victim and other participants are told that the lights will be turned off to assure some degree of privacy and that they will be turned on as soon as the first man reaches his goal. In total darkness, all the males pat their stomachs to simulate the sound of beating off. Suddenly the lights are turned on and only the victim is found to have phallus in hand and is actually jacking off.

Consider the terms used to describe solo sex. Most of the synonyms for masturbation seem to be saturated with humorous intent. A partial list would include the two most common phrases, "jacking off" and "jerking off." The word "masturbation" is far down the list in terms of its usage, and many males well versed in how it's done do not even know the word. Slang words depicting masturbation show its humorous aspect. Consider the following:

Beating one's meat, beating off, or simply beating it, J-O, whacking off, hand job, a trick with one's wick, a tryst with one's fist, pounding it, playing the skin flute, sliding one's trombone, solo on one's oboe (or piccolo), fisting it, flogging it, flailing it, pulling it. These are but a few of the commonly accepted slang terms with which just about all men are familiar.

Onanism, from the biblical character named Onan, is a synonym for masturbation, but it's all a mistake. Onan actually practiced coitus interruptus, withdrawing his penis just before ejaculation and spilling his seed on the ground—for which God struck him dead.

Curiously, although solo sex brings great pleasure, we often use the term disparagingly—as we do with coitus, for example, when we say, "Fuck you." When one man is seriously feeding another a line of preposterous nonsense, the listener may exclaim: "Are you trying to jerk me off?" When a man offers a friend a condition in which the friend is obviously the loser, a common retort is: "What kind of a jerk-off deal is this anyway?"

Apparently, when we take advantage of another, we don't just pull his leg.

Undoubtedly males have been jacking off since prehistoric times. The only thing that seems to have changed is people's attitudes about this generally solitary practice. For example, fathers and grandfathers remember stories about going blind, softening of the brain, having their cocks fall off, and going insane from masturbation. Today's young men find such superstition laughable.

No longer do we entertain the idea that a man is allotted a thousand orgasms in his lifetime and that none should be wasted through beating off. Now, even Boy Scout manuals no longer rile against the practice of solo sex with their former prudish, pussyfooting, and hilarious language.

In the 1990's, only a few neurotic, privately-guilty or psychologically impotent moralistic pundits ever gather sufficient audacity to suggest genuine or scientifically established vile consequences from masturbating. Mechanical devices, heavy mittens, male chastity belts, and even straight jackets designed to keep a young man's hands off his cock are now valuable only as museum pieces—or would be if curators would have the courage to display them.

Not only have knowledge and attitudes about beating off changed greatly during this century, but words used to describe it have undergone significant change. No longer do we hear about "self-abuse" or "self-defilement," whose connotation alone was enough to put at least some fear into a young man who was trying to cope with his sexuality. "Self-pollution" is gone, as is "that dirty habit."

Probably the major negative social factor still associated with sexual self-stimulation results from machismo: man the ravisher of women, man the beast whose sexual appetite is solely heterosexual, man whose sexuality would be somewhat disgraced were he to admit to jacking off instead of having sex with a woman. But, interestingly enough, even these men in their self-deception always seem to enjoy joking about other men beating off.

And, in general, women don't help the situation. Many females vehemently resent the fact that a man can satisfy his own sexual desires. Such an idea could easily lead some women to feel rejection. Mothers, rather than fathers, are far more punitive when they catch their sons masturbating or find those tell-tale "pecker tracks" on the sheets. That's probably why males, not females, find humor in jerk-off pranks or jokes about it—and why they seldom discuss masturbation with females, regardless of how close the relationship.

So, here it is—a joyous sex act found among virtually all males from puberty onward. They hold in their hands—literally—the secret to indescribable bliss. It's a truth that they can share, in general, with no women and few men without risking their macho image.

But we cannot be silent about this secret. It is to be celebrated—and mankind has found a way. Humor is the answer: *The Solo Sex Joke Book*.

To my knowledge, this is the first ever collection of solo sex humor. I encourage you to submit to the publisher your own favorites if they don't appear in these pages.

And now—enjoy!

—Ralph Mead PhD.

"Wow, 754 days of solitary confinement.
What'd you do to pass the time?"

YOUTH

Secret's Out

Some college men were having a bull session, and, as usual, the topic very quickly got around to sex. All of the men were eager participants and tried to share their sexual experiences and exploits with their buddies. Each had a storehouse of information, and all were eager to tell their tales in the most extravagant way they could.

It wasn't long before the discussion turned to the variations in male genitalia. Each succeeding story was more elaborate than the ones that went before.

Intending to top the others, one of the men announced that his roommate had a dick that was more than nine inches long. All the others were greatly impressed, so much so that one of them exclaimed,: "Can you beat that?"

"Well," came the reply, "I have—but I don't want to talk about it."

Who's Left?

The preacher had worked himself into a copious sweat as his frenzied sermon on the evils of sex became more and more animated and graphic. At the climax, he threw back his head and, flailing his arms wildly, shouted, "Now, I want all you folks in the congregation who have been he'in and she'in out of holy wedlock to get up from your pews and walk right out of this church."

Looking very sheepish, several of those who had been listening to the sermon got up and walked out.

"And now," continued the preacher, "I want every man who has been he'in and she'in with other men's wives to get up and walk right out that front door into the street where you belong." About half the remaining men stood and walked out.

"And now, all you women who have been he'in and she'in with other women's husbands, get up and walk right out behind those others," ranted the preacher. Many of the women got up and left the church.

"And now, it's your turn," continued the preacher. "All of you men who have been he'in and he'in and all you women who have been she'in and she'in—get up right now and get out of this church!" With this command, the remainder of the congregation walked out, leaving just one lone young man sitting in a front pew.

"Well now, sonny," said the preacher, wiping his brow, "it looks like it is just you and me who are the only righteous ones left who don't carry the heavy burden of sexual sin."

To this remark, the young man responded, "But, Mr. Preacher, sir, you ain't said nothing yet about all those who's been me'in and me'in."

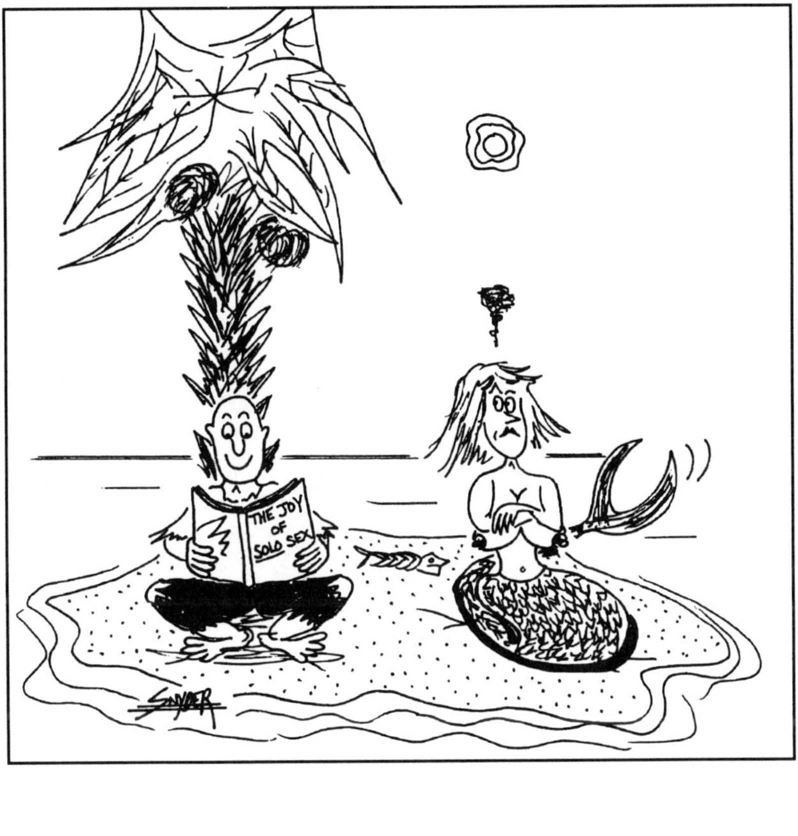
THE JOY OF SOLO SEX
SNYDER

"Around here, *every* Sunday is Palm Sunday!"

What's in a Word?

The family had been called to come to dinner. When all had been seated, Johnny unzipped his fly, pulled out his dick, and started to masturbate.

"*What in hell are you doing?*" asked his father. "The dinner table is no place for you to be doing a thing like that. If you *have* to do it, at least wait until bed time!"

"All I know," replied Johnny," is, my health teacher said if we want good digestion, we gotta masticate slowly every time we eat."

What's that?

Sister to brother who shares the same bedroom: "I think I hear somebody coming."

Happens All the Time

Brother Bob and brother Kirk
Grabbed and wrestled cousin Dirk.
Soon their projections—
Stupendous erections—
Led to a great circle jerk.

A Great Gift, If You Ask Me

A very frugal father asked his son what he would like to have as a gift for his birthday. The son pondered the question for a few moments and said he'd like new clothes and something to play with. The next day, the father bought his son a new pair of pants and cut holes in the pockets.

Definition

Mother: You've been in that bathroom for an hour, Johnny. We're packed and ready to leave. Are you coming?

Son: Not yet, Mom—but I'm breathing hard!

**"When you said you were a 'do-it-yourself'
kind of guy, I thought you could fix things!"**

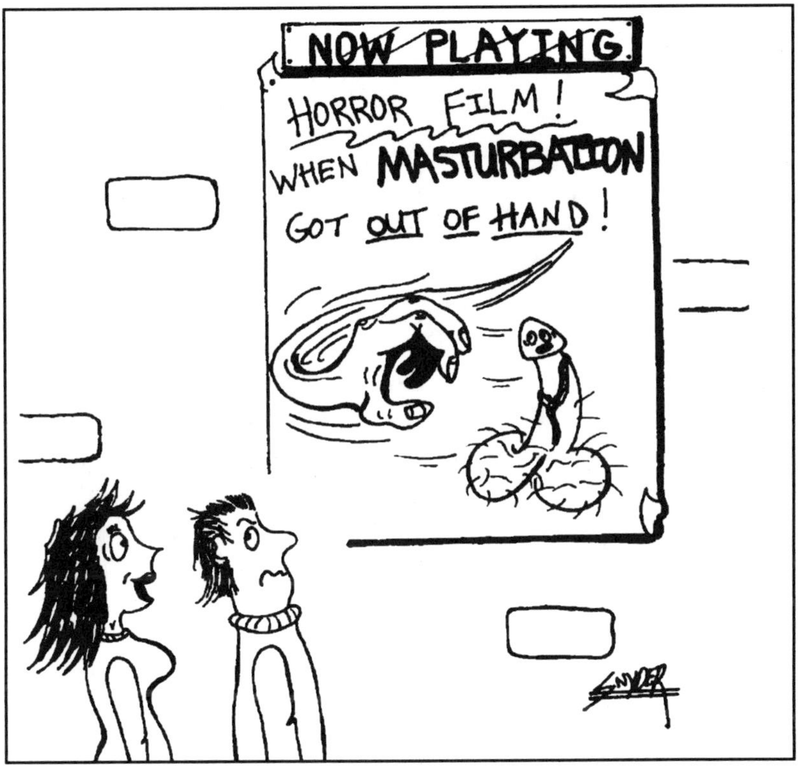
NOW PLAYING
HORROR FILM!
WHEN MASTURBATION
GOT OUT OF HAND!
SNYDER

"That's my significant other."

The Cure

Billy's family was becoming concerned because every time he urinated, he managed to dribble on his pants, leaving a tell-tale wet spot near his fly. Several techniques to prevent this embarrassing situation were tried, but none seemed to work. Finally, his father hit upon an idea and presented it to his son.

"Billy," he said, "I think we can solve this whole thing if every time you have to take a leak, you do it by the numbers." To demonstrate, he took his son into the bathroom and proceeded with his instruction. "When you want to take a leak, count off each step as you go—like this:

"1. Pull down your zipper.

"2. Take your peter out of your pants.

"3. Pull your foreskin all the way back.

"4. Now go ahead and take a leak.

"5. Carefully shake the last few drops off your peter.

"6. Push your foreskin back up over the end.

"7. Put your peter back in your pants and pull up your zipper."

Billy thought doing it by the numbers a very good idea. He proceeded to practice for a few weeks.

One day, when Billy went into the bathroom, his father decided to check up on his son's progress. He listened at the door. At first, all he could hear was a faint murmur from inside the bathroom. Moving closer, however, he heard the rapidly repeated words, "three-six, three-six; three-six; three-six…"

Solosexual

Now this young man from L.A.
Jacked off twelve times a day
As each pull and yank
Enriched the sperm bank
His fist was one hell of a "lay."

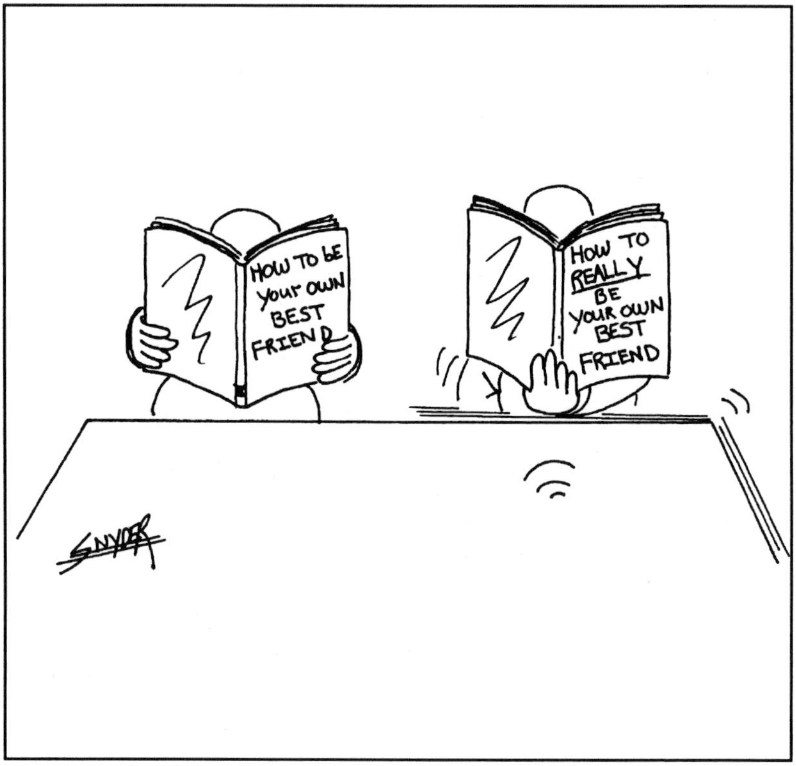
HOW TO bE your OWN BEST FRIEND
HOW TO REALLY BE YOUR OWN BEST FRIEND
SNYDER

Marriage

Setting Things Straight

A father was counseling his son on the eve of his marriage about how to make his marital life a great success. "Son," said the father, "there are three things that you must demonstrate for your bride right off, and the sooner you do them the better. First of all, demonstrate to her your physical strength. Second, show her you are a real man. And third, make sure she knows that you are completely independent."

A few weeks later the father met the son and inquired about how things were going now that he was married.

"Dad, you were quite right," said the son. "I followed your advice exactly and everything is going well. Here's what I did. On my wedding night, I picked up my new wife and carried her across the threshold to show her my strength. Then, to show her my manhood, I dropped my pants and briefs so she could have a good look. Finally, to demonstrate my independence, I lay down on the bed and jacked off."

Voodoo Dick

There was a businessman who was getting ready to go on a long business trip. He knew his wife was a flirtatious sort, so he thought he'd try to get something to keep her occupied while he was gone, because he didn't much like the idea of her screwing someone else.

So he went to a store that sold sex toys and talked to the old man behind the counter. He explained his situation. The old man said, "Well, I don't really know of anything that will do the trick. We have vibrating dildos, special attachments, and so on, but I don't know of anything that will keep her occupied for weeks, except..." and he stopped. "Except what?" the man asked.

"Well, sir, I don't usually mention this, but there is the 'voodoo dick.'" The old man reached under his counter and pulled out an old wooden box, carved with strange symbols. He opened it, and there lay a very ordinary looking dildo. The businessman laughed, and said, "Big deal. It looks like the other dildos in the shop!" The old man replied, "But you haven't seen what it'll do yet." He pointed to the door and said, "Voodoo dick, the door."

The voodoo dick rose out of its box, darted over to the door, and started screwing the keyhole, The old man said, "Voodoo dick, get back in your box!" The voodoo dick stopped, floated back to the box and lay there, quiescent once more.

"I'll take it!" said the businessman. The old man resisted, saying it wasn't for sale, but he finally surrendered to $700.00 in cash.

The guy took it home to his wife, told her it was a special dildo and that to use it, all she had to do was say, "Voodoo dick, my pussy." He left on his trip satisfied that things would be fine while he was gone.

After he'd been away a few days, the wife was getting unbearably horny. She thought of several people who would willingly satisfy her, but then she remembered the voodoo dick. She got it out, and said, "Voodoo dick, my pussy!"

The voodoo dick shot to her crotch and started pumping. It was great, like nothing she'd ever experienced before. After three orgasms, she decided she'd had enough, and she tried to pull it out, but it was stuck in her, still thrusting. She tried and tried to get it out, but nothing worked. Her husband had forgotten to tell her how to shut it off. So she decided to go to the hospital to see if they could help. She put her clothes on, got in the car and started to drive to the hospital, quivering with every thrust of the dildo. Suddenly another orgasm nearly made her swerve off the road, and she was pulled over by a policeman. He asked for her license, and then asked how much she'd had to drink.

Gasping and twitching, she explained that she hadn't been drinking, but that a voodoo dildo was stuck in her pussy, and wouldn't stop screwing.

The officer looked at her for a second and said, "Yeah, right. Voodoo dick my ass!"

Daily Chores

A 17-year-old farm boy was caught by his father jerking off behind the barn. "Son," the father said, "we've got to get you hitched so your wife can take care of that for you."

A while later, the young man married a buxom farm girl named Maybelle. For a time, everything seemed to be going well, but six months after the wedding the father caught his son again out behind the barn beating his meat.

"Son," the exasperated father shouted, "Maybelle is supposed to be taking care of that need for you."

The young man looked up from his task and replied, "She does, but her arm gets tired."

**"I don't expect *you* to figure it out—you
don't have a brain.**

Maturity

Goners

Psychiatrist: Please tell me all about your problem, young man.

Patient: Well, Doc, I seem to have this terrific compulsive disease. There's nothing I can do to stop.

Psychiatrist: And what is this disease or compulsion that is causing you so much anguish?

Patient: Well, I masturbate just about every day.

Psychiatrist: Hell, man, if that's a disease, I'm *dying* of it!"

How Many Men Does It Take To Screw in a Light Bulb While Masturbating?

Just one. But it takes the entire emergency room staff to get it back out.

Beach Stroker

There's a remote beach just north of L.A.
Where I go to relax for a day
As I lie in the sand
with my cock in my hand
I just stroke my stresses away.

Too Tight

What's the difference between red and purple?
Your grip.

The Ideal Partner

The great thing about being solosexual is that I know I'm going to make out with someone intelligent.

I Like Me Best

Sex, said Ricardo, is neater—
Indeed, it's quite a bit sweeter—
It's most consequential—
And quite confidential—
Between my left fist and my peter.

Speaking the Truth

Husband: Business is really bad. We have to cut back on expenses. You're going to have to learn to cook. I'm going to fire the chef.

Wife: I wish you'd stop jerking off and learn to screw so I could fire the chauffeur.

"It's his final statement."

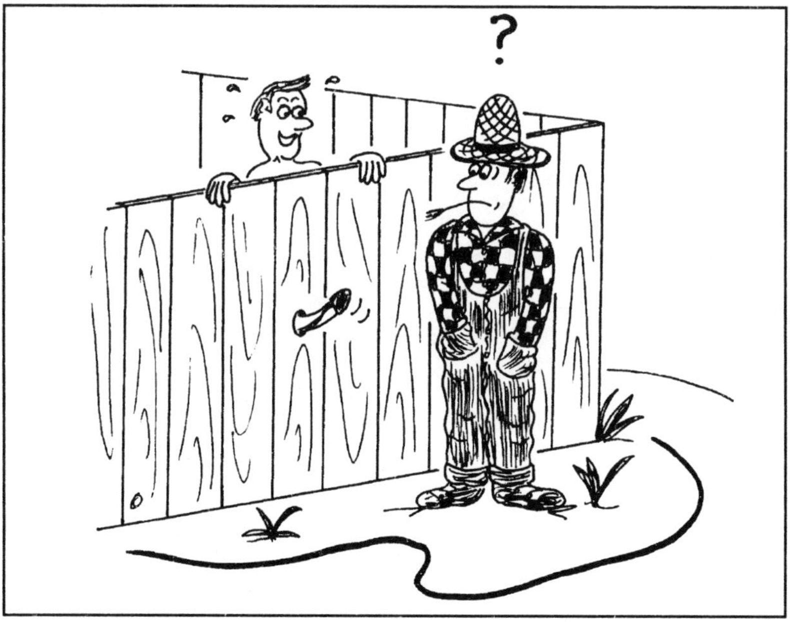
?

"*Please* jerk it off!"

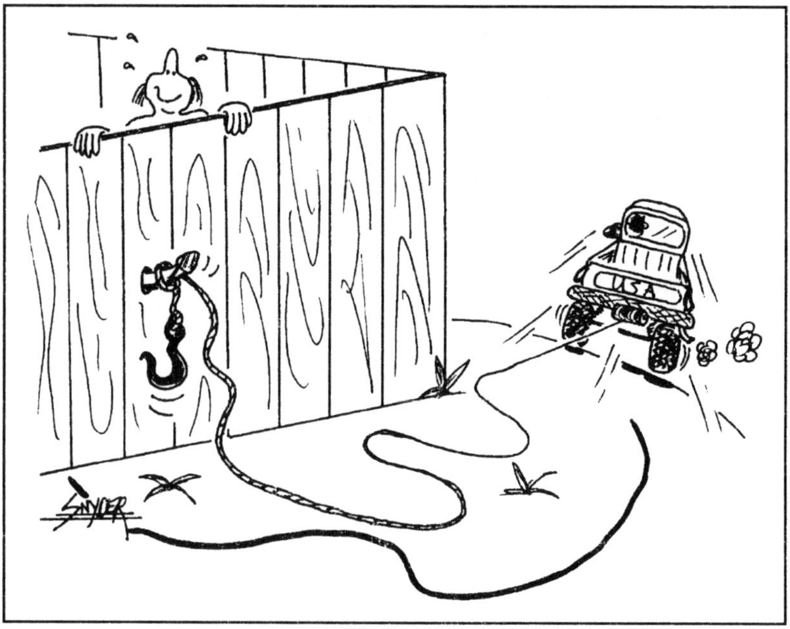
USA
SNYDER

Why Masturbation is the Best Sex

You need to buy only one dinner.

You don't have to go home in the morning.

You don't have to get dressed up.

You don't need to shower first.

There are no complaints if you fall asleep right after.

After your orgasm, you don't have to satisfy anyone else.

You May be a Confirmed Solosexual if...

At the height of orgasm you cry out your own name.

You use hair conditioner in the pubic area.

When you wave, instead of moving your hand left to right, it's up and down.

You're planning a vacation to Las Vegas, where, in a quickie ceremony, you can officially marry your dick.

When asked, "How's it hanging?" you point out that *he* has a *name*.

Every time you hear the term "main squeeze," your dick spasms.

You *know* your penis loves you back.

Into Horses

This guy goes to his psychiatrist and says, "You've gotta help me, doctor. I've got a compulsion to masturbate while petting horses."

So the kind-hearted doctor says, "Well, now, are you attracted to male horses or female horses?"

The guy snaps, "*Female* horses! What do you think I am—queer?"

The Difference

Question: What's the difference between "hard" and "light"?

Answer: Anyone can fall asleep with a light on.

"Kendall, get some contracts ready—we've got a winner!"

"Call me a *nut*, but it seems you've been quite testi lately."

"Just when you think you've seen it all..."

Take it—It's Yours

A Texan went into a sidewalk pissoir in Paris and proceeded to use the communal urinal inside. When he had finished and was shaking the last few drops off the end of his dick, he started to become sexually aroused. In a few seconds, his eight-inch erection demanded attention.

A Frenchman suddenly walked in and stopped dead in his tracks. With eyes bulging he exclaimed, "Mon dieu, Monsieur! With a ding-ding like that, you must be an American, I am thinking—no?"

When the American said that he was from Texas, the Frenchman continued. "S'il vous plait, Monsieur, just let me say that you have the most magnificent ding-ding I have ever seen!"

Even though the American was both astonished and confused, he could not help but feel flattered as well. He decided that the French were quite open in matters having to do with sex and sexual equipment.

The American acknowledged the compliment, and the Frenchman continued. "And, Monsieur, would you mind letting me have the great honor of touching your ding-ding so I might know how it feels in my hand?"

Even more astonished this time, the American nonetheless did not want to seem prudish and offend the Frenchman. After all, he thought, when in Rome do as the Romans do. So he allowed his new French acquaintance to handle his cock.

"Oh, Monsieur, now your ding-ding is making hard. Oh, so hard. So very, very hard--just like iron rod—no?" exclaimed the Frenchman. "Ooh-la-la, such a nice big and hard ding-ding. Now I do for you—how is it you say—make the jerk him for you, yes?"

By this time, the American was indeed becoming well aroused and so he allowed his new French friend to start stroking his cock.

After several vigorous strokes, the Frenchman said, "And Monsieur, I think you must also have a very beautiful pair of balls there in your pants? It would be so much more magnifique if I could just feel your balls in my other hand while I do the jerk-him for you with this one, yes?"

With all of this attention and stroking, the American was getting so excited that he eagerly presented his balls to his new acquaintance.

The Frenchman fondled the American's balls for a few seconds and then, as he took them firmly in the palm of his hand, announced, "And now, Monsieur, your wallet, please."

The Best

My penis, my pecker, my cock or my dick—
I beat it; I pound it; I jerk on my prick.
Whatever you call it,
To swing or to ball it,
My fist on my peter's my favorite trick.

Men's Night Out

Several married men were playing their weekend game of cards and decided to try "jerk-off poker" in which each man puts a dollar in the kitty and the one who ejaculates first wins the trophy and all the money. After a few minutes the referee called out, "O.K. you guys, everyone stop. Jason over in the corner has finished."

Since everyone but Mark stopped stroking, the referee called to him, "Mark, did you hear what I said? Jason has finished. Time to call it quits."

But as Mark kept on he said, "The game may be over, but I have such a good hand I'm playing through."

**"I don't understand it. Five hours,
and we haven't made a dime!"**

**"Look Gomez, Uncle Fester and "Thing"
play *so* well together."**

GAYS

A Reputation

Luigi stands on the shore overlooking the Bay of Naples and tells Fernando, "You see all those boats out there? I built every one of them. But do they call me Luigi the boat builder? No."

Luigi turns and gestures to the houses on the hillside behind him. "I built about half of those houses, Fernando, truly I did. But do they call me Luigi the house builder? No."

Discouraged, Luigi sits down in the sand. "But let me suck just one cock, Fernando, and..."

Friendship

Here's to my good buddy Enos.
We share masturbation between us.
Whenever we meet
And proceed to greet,
We grab for each other's penus.

Helping the Widow

Farmer Jones died during the winter, and when it came time for spring planting, Widow Jones realized she couldn't do all the work herself. So she applied to the town council, only to be told that all able-bodied farmhands had already been hired and the only one left was gay. Widow Jones chose him and was pleased to find him a steady and reliable worker. When six weeks of hard labor had gone by, the man asked Widow Jones if he could have Saturday night off to go into town.

"All right," she consented, "but be back by nine o'clock."

The farmhand wasn't back until ten-thirty, and then he tiptoed up the stairs. A moment later, Widow Jones threw open the door to discover him masturbating. "How wasteful!" she exclaimed. "Take off my shoes," she commanded. He obeyed. "Take off my dress." He did so. "Take off my slip...and stockings...and my garter belt."

The gay farmhand obeyed without saying a word.

"Now take off my bra," snapped Widow Jones, "and don't you ever borrow my clothes again!"

What A Night!

Three straight college buddies decide to go skiing one weekend. When they reach the resort, they discover that only one room is still available, although it has a king-sized bed. Exhausted, they all strip, hit the sack and fall to sleep immediately. The next morning, the guy on the right of the bed says, "I had this wild, vivid dream of getting a hand job. It seemed to last all night!" The guy on the left says the same, and points to dried semen on his abdomen. The guy in the middle sits up in amazement.

"I feel cheated. All I dreamed about was cross country skiing. I poled clear across Alaska!"

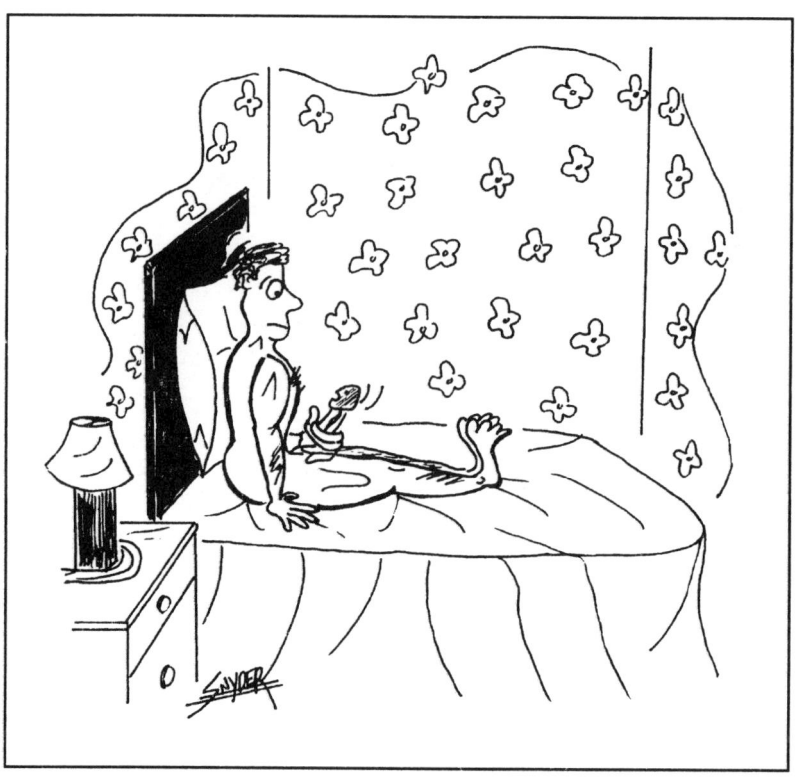

"At least you could try some foreplay first!"

"Whose turn is it tonight?"

"That's *not* what self-service means!"

"Yeah, when I get home my owner's gonna beat me too."

HILLBILLIES AND REDNECKS

On the Railroad

Grandpa and Grandma, Mother and Father, and their son Tom all had to sleep in one room.

One night after all had gone to bed and the lights were out, Grandpa whispered to Grandma, "Would you like to have it fast like a passenger train or slow like a freight train?" Grandma did not hesitate to reply that she wanted it slow like a freight train.

Soon thereafter, Father said to Mother, "Would you like to have it fast like a passenger train or slow like a freight?" Mother, too, was very decisive and said she wanted it fast like a passenger train.

A few minutes later, Tom's bed started bouncing up and down and squeaking. "Whatever is going on over there?" asked his father.

"I'm doing it like a hand-car," Tom gasped, "And I'm just about over...the...*hill!*"

Buckshot Stew

A man was cooking a stew for his three sons when he accidentally knocked over a can of buckshot, which fell directly into the stew. Not having time to fish it all out, he decided to serve the stew as it was.

The next day, one of his sons came rushing into the house and said with great concern, "Dad, you won't believe this, but all day long I have been shitting these little bee-bees." His father calmed him and explained the accident.

A few minutes later, the second son appeared, equally anxious, and with the same story. Again, the father explained the reasons for his son's problem.

A short time later, the third son rushed into the house. He was crying hysterically and could hardly talk.

"I know what you're going to tell me that —you've been shitting buck-shot all day," the father said.

"No," wailed the son. "I was out to the garage jacking off, and when I came, I shot the dog!"

Never Mind

A man walked into a fishery headquarters office to apply for a job he'd heard advertised on the radio. During the employment interview, the officer asked the applicant if he could demonstrate his skills.

"I'd be glad to," announced the man, standing. He dropped his pants and briefs, grabbed his dick and started jacking off.

"Put your pants back on and get out of here, you idiot," shouted the employment officer. "We don't want that kind of thing going on around here. We advertised for a master *baiter.*"

Rednecks Don't Masturbate

How do rednecks have safe sex in Alabama?

They spray paint the flanks of all the sheep that kick.

"Masturbation *is* a 'touchy' subject Joey, which is precisely why I ordered this instructional video series. Let's see—*"Debbie Does Dallas,"* "Deep Throat,"***...**

"Well, that explains why you've been thinking with the head of your dick."

People of the Earth

A traveling salesman's car broke down in front of a farmhouse in a very remote part of the countryside. Noting that there were no other signs of life for miles around, he knocked on the door and asked if he could stay at the farmer's house overnight.

The farmer thought for a moment and said, "Well, yes you can. But the only place I have for you to sleep is in the same room with my young daughter here." Although the salesman was accustomed to much more privacy, he agreed, seeing that he had no other choice.

As the salesman and farmer's daughter were undressing for bed, the daughter saw something hanging between the man's legs she had never seen before. She asked him what it was. Embarrassed, the salesman stammered for a moment, but finally said, "That's my dolly. I play with it now and then just like you play with your doll." With this interchange, the two got into bed and went to sleep.

A few hours later, the salesman was awakened by sobbing from the bed next to his. Turning on the light, he found the farmer's daughter crying, her sobs literally rocking the bed. The salesman asked what troubled her.

"Oh, Mister, I'm so sorry," she sobbed. "It is so sad. I was playing with your dolly and decided to give it a massage and a back rub. The first thing I knew, your dolly sat up. Then it threw up. And now, I think it's dead."

Sorry City Slicker

A man from the city was visiting his cousin, who operated a dairy farm. When showed the milking machine, the city man's eyes lit up.

"I bet that thing can give a hell of a blow job!" he exclaimed. His farmer cousin agreed, and offered to help get him hooked up to the machine.

A few minutes later, after having experienced one of the very best orgasms of his life, the city man called to his cousin, "That's enough. You can turn it off now."

The farmer shook his head and smiled. "It shuts off automatically after twenty gallons."

Jack Off

If Jack will help Jill off a horse, will Jill help Jack off a horse?

Traveling Salesman

A traveling salesman out in the country had finished his rounds for the day and was headed back to the city. He noticed that the sky was getting really dark and that a bad storm was coming up. He knew that he could not make it back to the city before the storm hit, so he stopped at a nearby farmhouse and asked the farmer if he could spend the night. The farmer said, "Sure, but you will have to sleep with my son in the attic".

The traveling salesman said, "Great." After dinner they all got up and went to their rooms to go to bed. The salesman and the farmer's son went up to the attic. The salesman got undressed and jumped into bed. The farmer's son put on his pajamas and knelt down beside the bed.

The salesman thought to himself, "Boy I sure am a bad influence on this kid," so he jumped out of bed and knelt down beside the boy.

The kid looked over at the salesman and asked "What you doing, mister?"

The salesman said, "I'm doing the same thing your doing".

The little boy looked back over at the salesman and said, "Well, you better not let Ma see you doing it over there— the pot's over here."

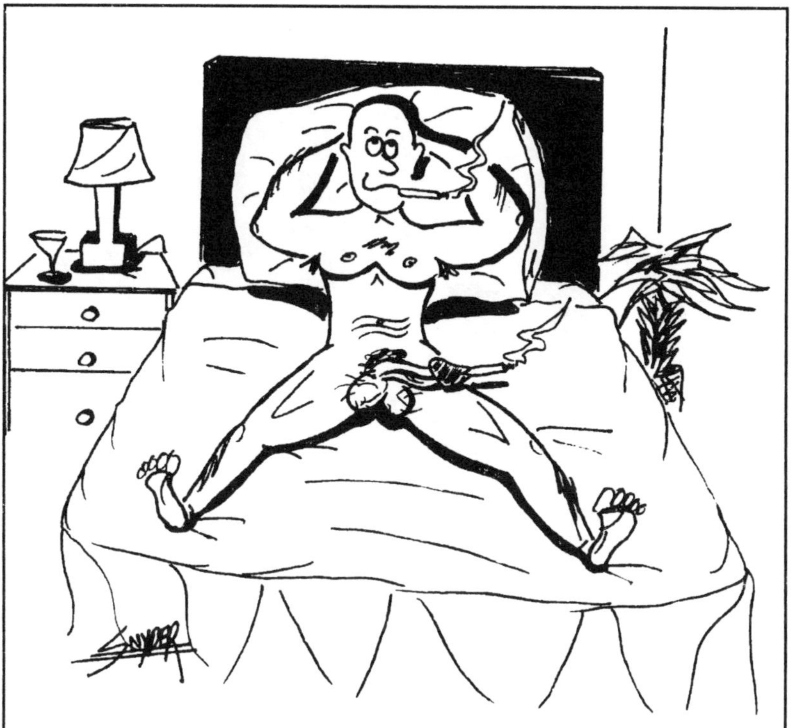
SNYDER

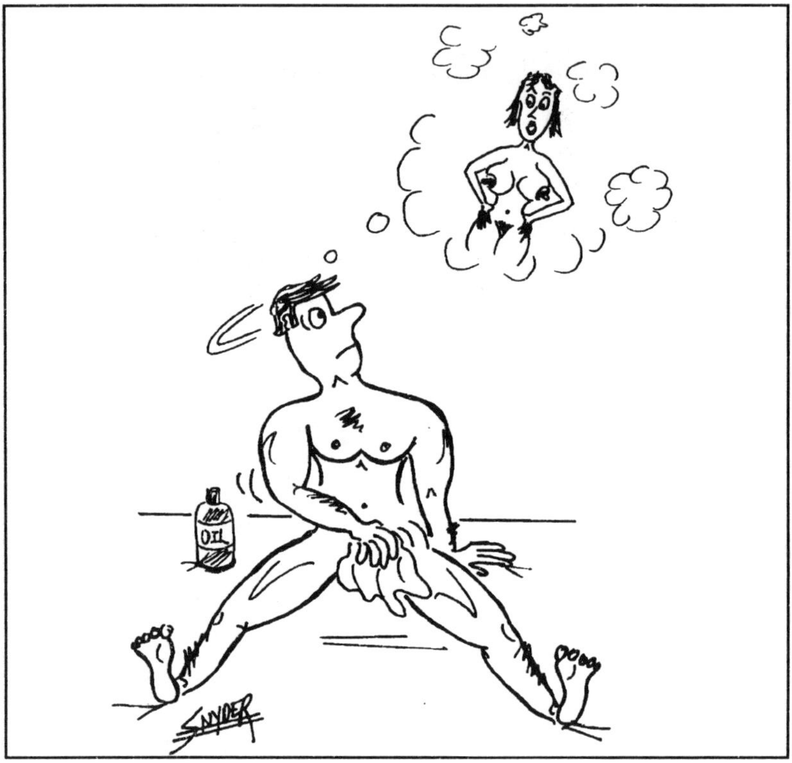
OIL
SNYDER

"You're doing *what*?"

MISCELLANEOUS

A Problem at the Sperm Bank

A ninety-year-old man went to the sperm bank and told the nurse that he wanted to make a donation. Although more than a little surprised at the request, she handed him a bottle and told him to go into the men's room and produce the specimen.

An hour passed, and then nearly two hours. Finally, the nurse became alarmed, opened the door a crack and called in to the old man, "Are you having any difficulty in there?"

The old man called back, "Hell, yes, I'm having trouble. I pulled it, stroked it and banged it on the toilet seat. I pounded it and bashed it against the wash basin for almost half an hour. Finally, I tried grabbing it and rubbing it all the way around the top-but I'll be damned if I can get the top off this bottle!"

Dictionary Definition

Masturbation—Making oneself at home.

Down at the Drug Store

A fifteen-year-old boy is browsing through *Playboy* in the magazine section of the local pharmacy when he spots a middle-aged man approach the clerk at the store's check-out counter. Listening carefully, he hears the man say, "I need a large supply of condoms, but I'm not sure what size."

As the boy watches, the woman reaches into the man's pants. Then she picks up a microphone and says over the store's speakers, "Jake, I need a box of the extra large condoms at the check-out counter."

No sooner does the first man pay for his purchase and leave then another, somewhat younger, gentleman approaches the same clerk. This fellow says almost the exact same thing as the first man, and once again the woma
n reaches into his pants, feels her way around, and after a moment says into the microphone, "Jake, I need another box of extra large condoms at the check-out counter."

By now the young man's heart is pounding with excitement. Although red-faced with embarrassment, he walks boldly up to the counter and says, "Miss, I need a box of condoms, but I'm not sure what size I am."

His wildest dream comes true. She reaches into his pants, feels around, squeezes, then announces over the speaker, "Jake, we need a mop up here at the check-out counter."

Snob

A man to his friend: "Why do you jerk off so much? There are lots of sex partners out there."

"Right, but I meet a better class of people this way."

"He wants a bigger penis."

"Fortunately, the accident hasn't altered his lifestyle."

Charge of the Sperm Brigade

At the training camp for millions of vigorous, wiggly sperm inside the man's body, there was never time for rest. These sperm were being trained for their sole mission in life—to be the only one strong and clever enough to reach the egg and fertilize it. All of the others would be flushed away to drown. This fact made competition extremely fierce. Each was determined that he would be the one to claim victory. All of the sperm eagerly and nervously awaited the "red alert" signal which would announce the moment of attack.

From time to time there were false alarms caused when their host experienced a morning erection or a horny thought or two. Each time, however, the troops stood at attention and made ready for battle. And then the "at ease" command would sound. The battle was yet to be.

One day the red alert sounded much louder than before. This was it! The moment for the fateful charge had come. It was now or never. All the sperm mobilized and fell into ranks awaiting the signal to charge. Rank upon rank at full attention, all were in sustained readiness for the order to go forth to battle. The red alert grew even brighter and louder. Bells rang; sirens sounded. Excitement among the troops reached electric proportion. The atmosphere literally crackled with tension. At the moment when it seemed they could bear it no longer, a cannon fired and the order was shouted to charge.

Each sperm vowed that *he* would be victorious, and this increased the excitement as they collectively rushed forward. But it was the commanding officer of the sperm battalion who led the charge, whose resolve and hopes were greatest. It was he who was best trained and the most valiant of all. He was in a better position to reach the target than those who brought up the rear of the brigade.

All at once, propelled by the spastic force of the orgasm, the entire battalion of sperm was hurled relentlessly into a long, narrow tube. By this time, disarray had set in among the minor troops. Each sperm tried to push and shove his way to the front, but the commanding officer kept himself well out ahead of all the others. He led his army in a most masterful advance.

Suddenly, as the intelligence corps had foretold, there was light at the end of the long, hot and narrow tunnel. And then, just as suddenly, the lead sperm saw victory *snatched* away

"Halt! Retreat! Go back!" he shouted. "Save yourselves before it's too late. This one's a hand job!"

Captured Kleptic

A woman rushes up to a store detective and says, "Do you see that man over there? He just put something in his pocket." Both the woman and the detective approach the man. The woman charges, "I just saw you put something in your pocket."

"Did not."

Did so!" And with that, she slips her hand into the offending pocket. Whereupon she faints.

"What have you got in that pocket?" the detective demands.

"Pocket? Whose got pockets?"

Playing Games

Gay guy says to straight guy, "Let's play Hide and Seek. I'll hide and if you find me, I'll beat you off."

Straight guys says, "But what if I don't find you?"

Gay guy says. "I'll be behind the couch."

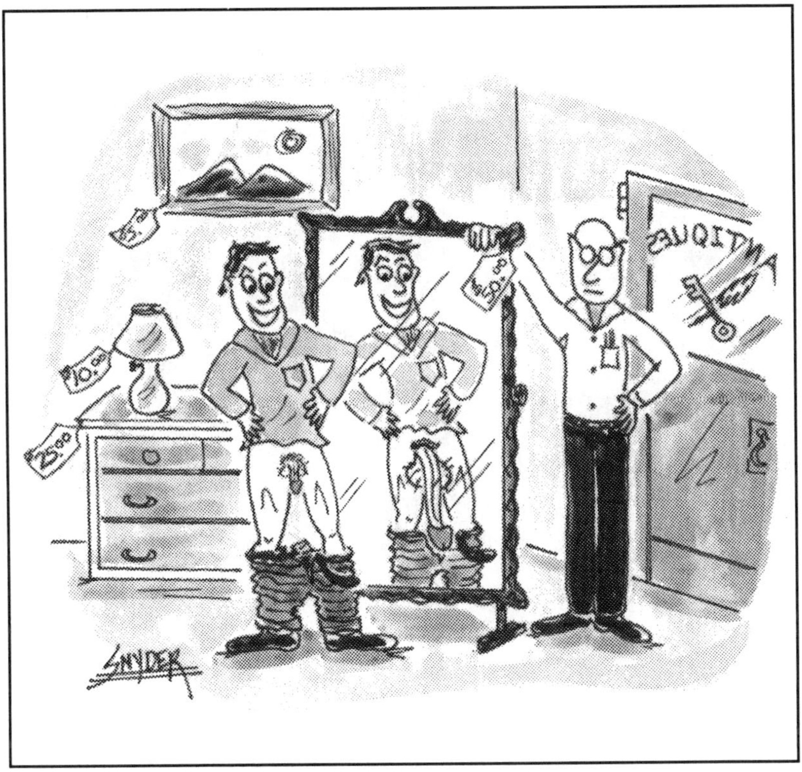
SNYDER

"I'll take it!"

"Poor bastards."

Fraternity Cheers

Fraternities and many other men's organizations have special songs for festive all-male occasions, generally when only the membership is within earshot. Here are a few examples of fraternity songs and cheers:

> Come, my brothers, let us go
> Grab your dicks and stoke 'em slow.
> Stroke 'em fast,
> Until at last
> We shoot our loads at old *Chi Rho.*

> Come, my brothers, grab your dicks;
> Aim them well at *Alpha X.*
> Shoot at *Theta,*
> Masturbata
> Blast them all beyond the Styx.

> Come, my brothers, drop your pants.
> Grab your peters with your hands.
> Pull on your masts
> And beat 'em fast
> And make our fraternity jump and dance.

And our brothers in Scotland have ballads which are a part of festivities which promote their camaraderie. These are usually sung while drinking or engaging in general horseplay, which is highly prized among the men of Scotland. The Scots like to poke fun at each other, and often the butt of their jokes has to do with the sexual equipment of their buddies. As with men of all cultures and countries, jacking off is a common topic. And you can be certain that the Scots have a special meaning when they wink at you and say they are going to play a tune on their "bagpipes."

Harken, me lads, whip em out;
Get a good grip on ye spout;
Pull back ye skin
Agin' and agin'
And blast wi' ye juice all-about.

MacTavish had yanked off his kilt
And got a good grip on his hilt;
His intention, ye see
Was not just to pee
But to see that his seedies were spilt.

Peter MacGregor, a Dundee bloke
Whacked his peter till his arm was broke.
Ever so wistful
With wonderful fistful
Jerked on his dick with a left-handed stroke.

Ivan McEwan of old Glasgow town
Known all about with some renown
Took out his elf
And played with himself
Pulling his skin up and down.

What Do People Mean...

When they say, "The computer went down on me"?

"Sure we can lick our balls, but we can't
Jerk Off!"

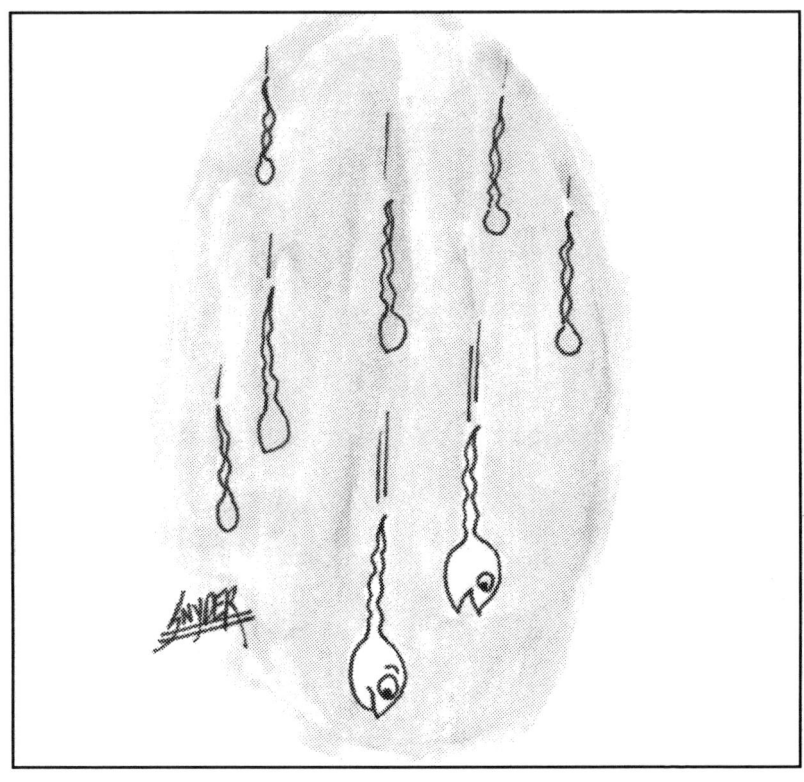

"Wow, whoever thought he'd do it off the edge of the Grand Canyon!"

Little Old Lady and the Bet

A little old lady went into the Bank of Canada one day, carrying a bag of money. She insisted that she must speak with the president of the bank to open a savings account because, "It's a lot of money!"

A few minutes later, the bank president asked her how much she would like to deposit. She replied, "$165,000!" and dumped the cash out of her bag onto his desk.

The president asked, "Where did you get this money?"

The old lady replied, "I make bets."

"Bets? What kind of bets?"

The old woman said, "Well, for example, I'll bet you $25,000 that your balls will be square by tomorrow."

"Ha!" laughed the president. "That's a stupid bet. You can never win that kind of bet!"

The old lady challenged, "So, will you take my bet?"

"Sure," said the president, "I'll bet $25,000 that my balls are not square!"

The little old lady then said, "Okay, but since there is a lot of money involved, may I bring my attorney for verification?"

"Sure!" replied the confident president.

The next morning at precisely 10:00 a.m., the little old lady appeared with her lawyer at the president's office. She introduced the lawyer to the president and repeated the bet: "$25,000 says the president's balls are square!"

The president agreed with the bet again and the old lady asked him to drop his pants so they could all see. The president complied. The little old lady peered closely at his balls. "I can't see well," she said. I've got to *feel* them."

"Well, okay," said the president, "$25,000 is a lot of money, so I guess you should be absolutely sure." As the little old lady fondled his testicles, the president noticed that the lawyer was quietly banging his head against the wall.

He asked the old lady, "What the hell's the matter with your lawyer?"

She replied, "Nothing, except I bet him $100,000 that at 10:00 a.m. today I'd have the bank president's balls in my hand."

Gepetto's Advice

When Pinocchio had sex with his girlfriend she complained, "I'm all full of splinters!"

So Pinocchio ran to Gepetto and told him the problem. Gepetto turned to his tool box and handed little Pinochhio a piece of sandpaper. Gleaming with gratitude, Pinocchio hurried home to sand his tool.

A few weeks later, Gepetto ran into Pinocchio on the street. "How's it going with your girlfriend?" he asked.

Pinocchio answered, "I'm sanding myself five times a day—who needs a girlfriend?"

Old Play on Words

A man riding the bus with his son called to the driver. "Sir, would you mind stopping at the next corner and let me and my son Jack off?"

Athlete

Hear ye the story of my buddy Pete.
Agree, if you will, he's quite an athlete.
He's most contemplative
And quite innovative.
He learned to jerk off with his feet.

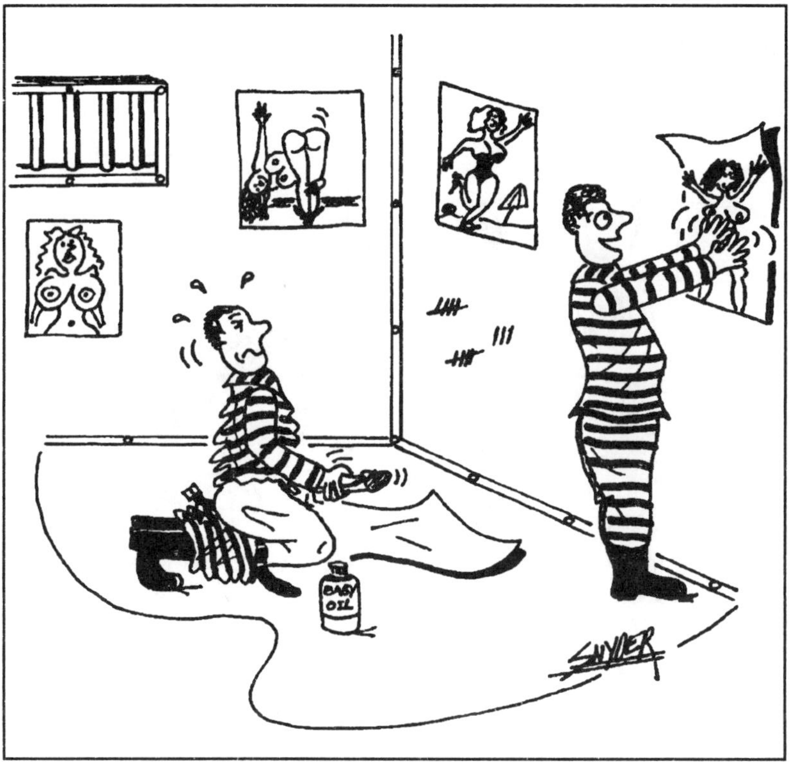
BABY OIL
SNYDER

"More glue. More glue!"

"It's sniffles and hemorrhoids, Edith—just sniffles and hemorrhoids. Common problem with teenage boys."

Questions of Profound Importance

What's worse than having your doctor tell you, you have
V.D.?
Having your dentist tell you.

What should you do if your girlfriend starts smoking?
Slow down and possibly use a lubricant.

What can a bird do that a man can't?
Whistle through his pecker.

What did the elephant say to the nude man?
Sure it's cute, but can if pick up peanuts?

What can jelly beans do that humans can't?
Come in different colors.

He: How many drinks does it take to make you dizzy?
She: Three, but the name is Daisy.

Why Is Chocolate Better Than Sex?

—"If you love me, you'll swallow" has real meaning
with chocolate.

—Chocolate satisfies even when it goes soft.

—You can eat chocolate even in front of your mother.

—If you bite the nuts too hard the chocolate won't mind.

—You don't get hairs in your mouth when you eat
chocolate.

—Chocolate doesn't make you pregnant.

—You can have as many chocolates as you want, any-
time, anywhere.

—With chocolate, size doesn't matter—it's always
good.

—Chocolate doesn't make you gag.

Steps in Overcoming Masturbation

When we saw this item in *Spy Magazine* recently, we thought it was a put-on. We spent time and money trying unsuccessfully to track down its origins. Then, we discovered Deoborah Laake's auto-biography *Secret Ceremonies*. In it, she refers to Mormon Church teachings relating to masturbation, "perhaps most unforgettably immortalized in a pamphlet written by a respected church leader during my adolescence..."

The following are excerpts from this pamphlet, written by Mark E. Petersen, along with our comments, of course:

"When the temptation to masturbate seems overwhelming, yell, 'Stop!' and recite a prechosen scripture **[not having anything to do with rods or staffs]**.

"Use aversion therapy—associate something very distasteful with your loss of self control. For example, if you are tempted to masturbate, think of having to bathe in a tub of worms, and eat several of them as you do the act. **[That may not keep you from masturbating, but it sure will get you to associate worms with kinky sex.]**

"During your toileting and shower activities, leave the bathroom door or shower curtain partly open to discourage being alone in total privacy. **[Who knows? You may not have to jerk yourself off after all. Hell, why not just walk around the house naked?]**

"Avoid people, situations, pictures or reading materials that may create sexual excitement. **[In other words, live in a coffin.]**

"It is sometimes helpful to have a physical object to use in overcoming this problem. A *Book of Mormon*, firmly held in hand, even in bed at night has proven helpful in extreme cases. **[If this really is supposed to work, wouldn't it be smarter to have a *Book of Mormon* in *both* hands?]**

"In very severe cases it may be necessary to tie a hand to the bed frame with a tie in order that the habit of masturbating in a semi-sleep condition can be broken. This can also be accomplished by wearing several layers of clothing which would be difficult to remove while half asleep." **[In extreme cases such as these, we recommend that eager masturbators diligently study Harold Litten's psychic orgasm techniques.]**

When Ya Gotta Go

While his mother was entertaining society ladies for lunch, little George blurted out, "I gotta pee!" His mother pulled him aside and said, "Next time, George, don't say pee, say I have to whisper."

George learned his lesson. That night, he went into his parents' room and shook his father. "Dad," he said, "I have to whisper."

His father responded, groggily, "Okay, George, whisper in my ear."

"You gonna eat them nuts, mister, or just play with them?"

"Come on Murray, you've got to admit, it's
a hell of a lot more entertaining than the
original version!"

"Um let's see... beat off... whack off... no wait—jack off... oh, honestly Frank, cum with it already!"

"Now this little baby is not only a watch, it also has a built-in strokometer."

"Believe me, you've never looked better!"

"It's not what you think, Mom. I'm just extending my...life span!"

What working hard is all about.

"What? A nice Catholic boy like you having sex with a *Baptist*?"

"That's Mr. Barnesworth. Every year he fires his one shot and then falls asleep."

"I think we're on the beatin' path, Harry."

"Yes, I can solve the problem—but it's not covered under Medicare."

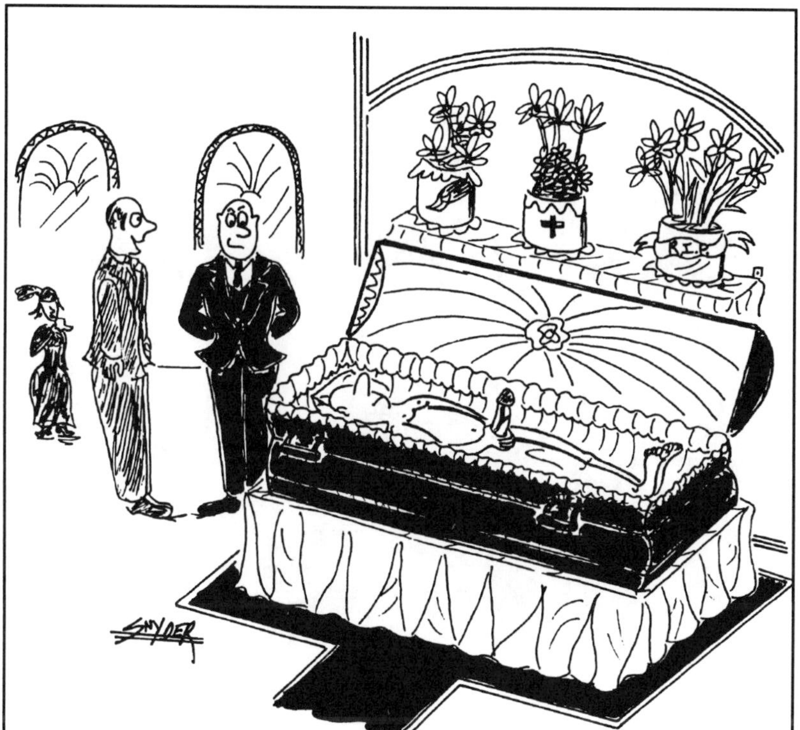
SNYDER
R.I.P.

"He was such a Jerk-off."

**"Davey's the class clown.
I'm the class jerk-off!"**

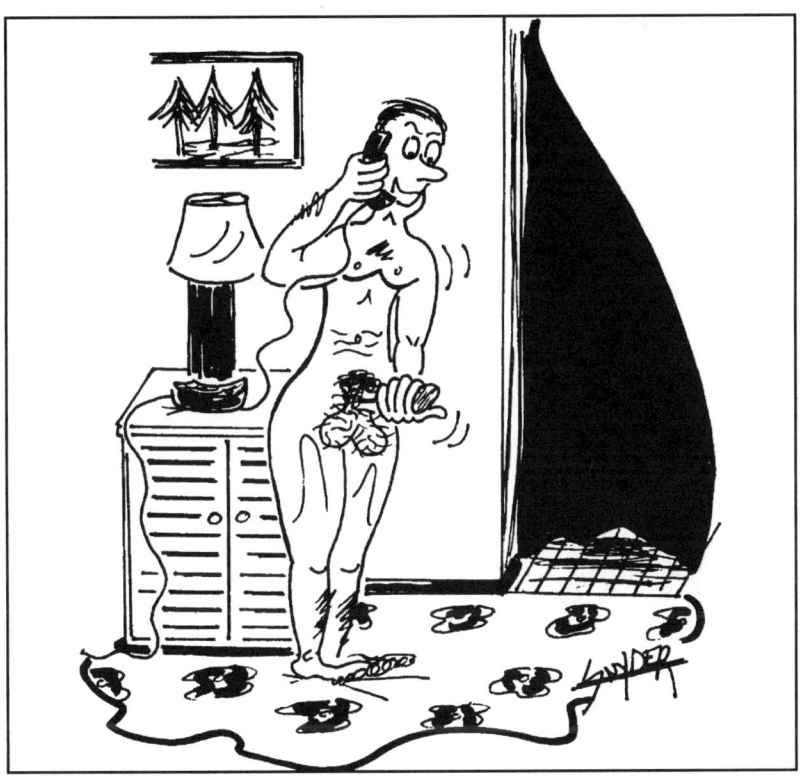

**"How are you doing? Oh me?
I'm holding my own..."**

THE ONGOING CARTOON CAPTION WRITING CONTESTS

We have another fifteen great cartoons by Christian Snyder—but we *hate* the captions, so we're not printing them. Instead, we'll pay $50.00 each for the best captions we can find. We at **FACTOR PRESS**, in our inimitable wisdom, will decide which is best.

We hope this book will be in print for a thousand years, but we know you don't want to wait that long to get your fifty bucks. So *Closing date for submission* to the first contest *is December 31, 1999.* If you're reading this on January 1, 2000, you'll have to enter the *second* contest, which closes June 30, 2000. And so on, until we go broke or get bored reading your captions.

You can tear the following fifteen pages out of this copy (if you own it), and buy another for its future skyrocketing value as a collector's item. Or you may photocopy the following cartoons and type or print your captions below the pictures. Please put your name and address on *each* picture. (And *don't* copy the rest of the book or we'll put you in the slammer for life for copyright violation, and you'll *really* learn about solo sex.) Send all entries to:

CARTOONS, FACTOR PRESS, PO Box 8888, Mobile, AL 36689

Yes, you may submit as many captions as you like—and you're eligible for more than one prize. Winners will be announced and checks mailed in February, 2000, and every six months thereafter—and you'll have a better chance with us than with Publishers Clearinghouse. If you'd like a list of winners, please send a stamped and self-addressed envelope with your submissions.

P.S. If we have to say you don't have to buy this book to enter this contest, we're saying it. Ha!

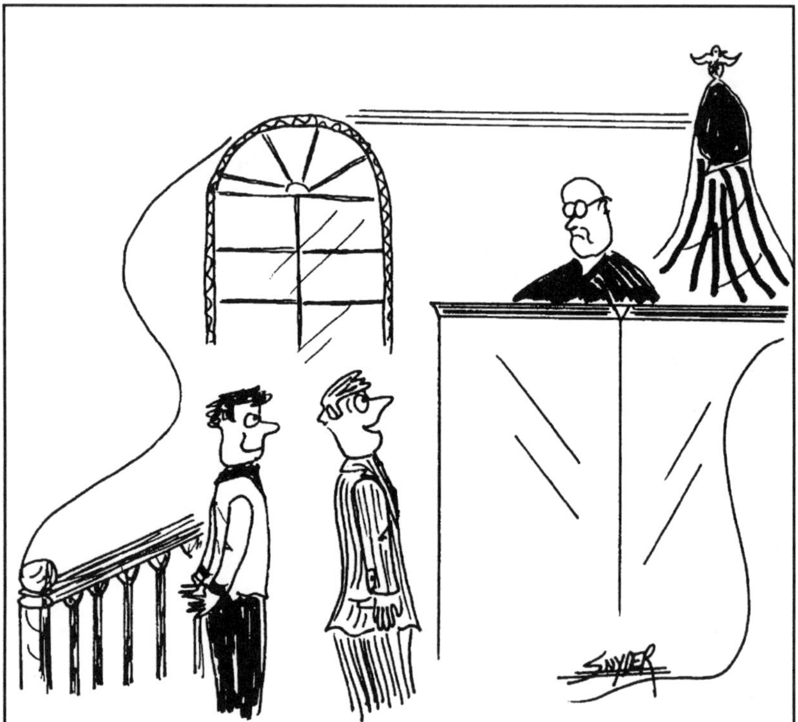
SNYDER

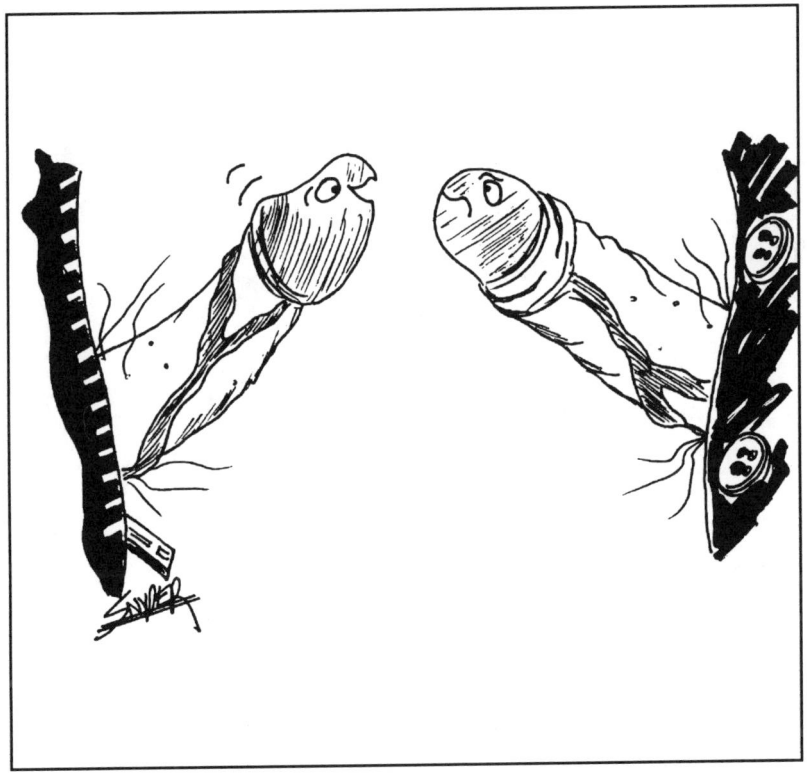

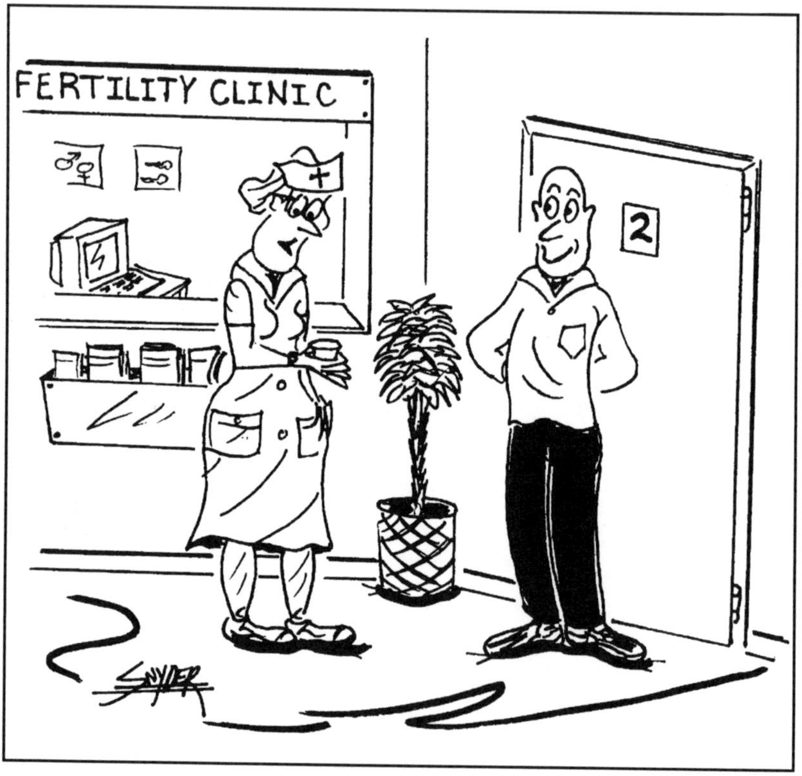
FERTILITY CLINIC
2
SNYDER

?
SNYDER

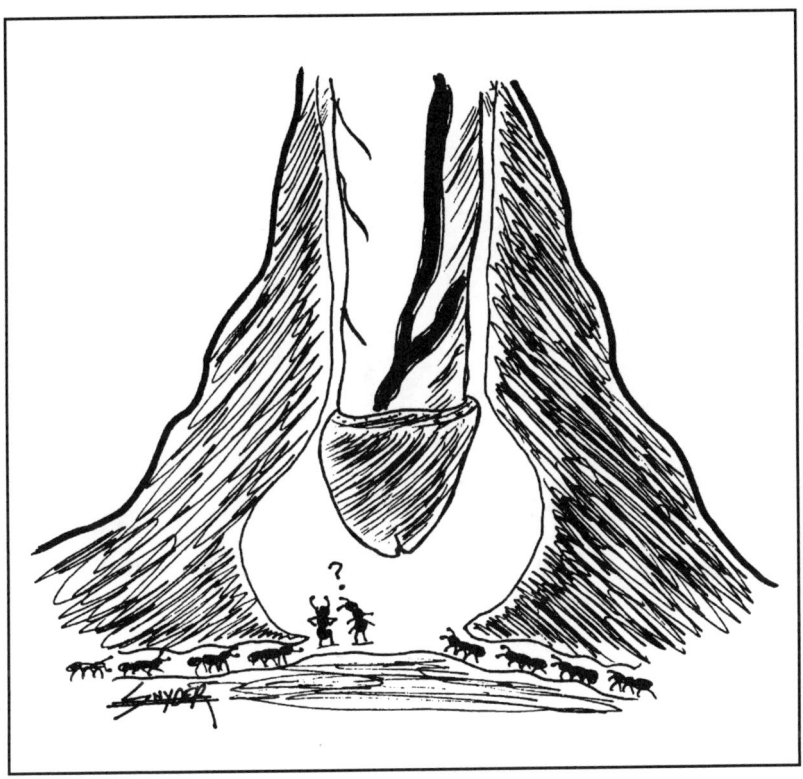

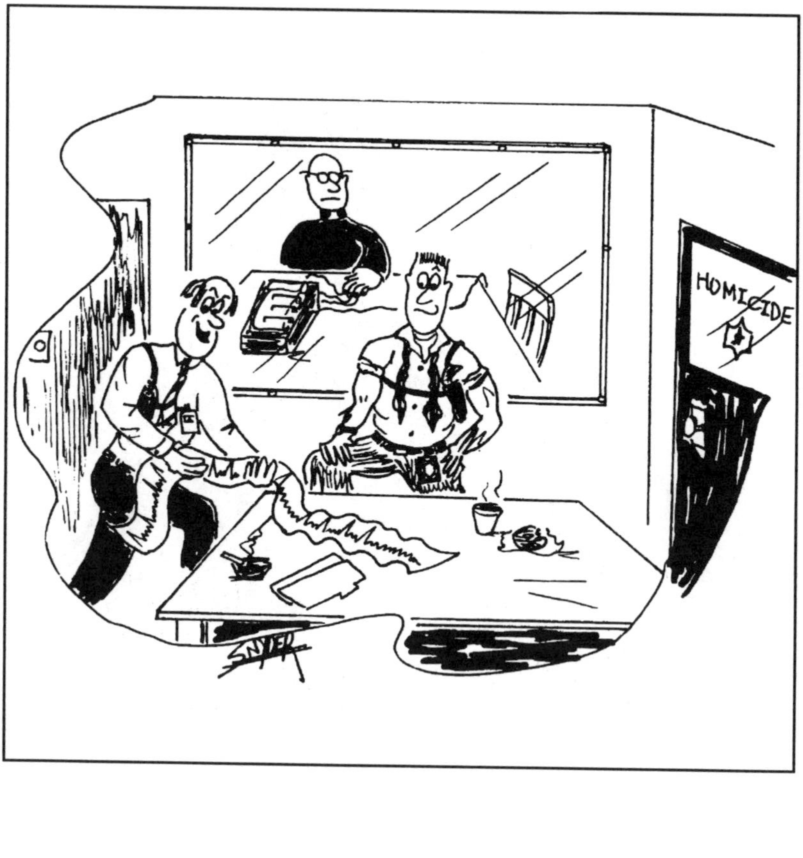
HOMICIDE

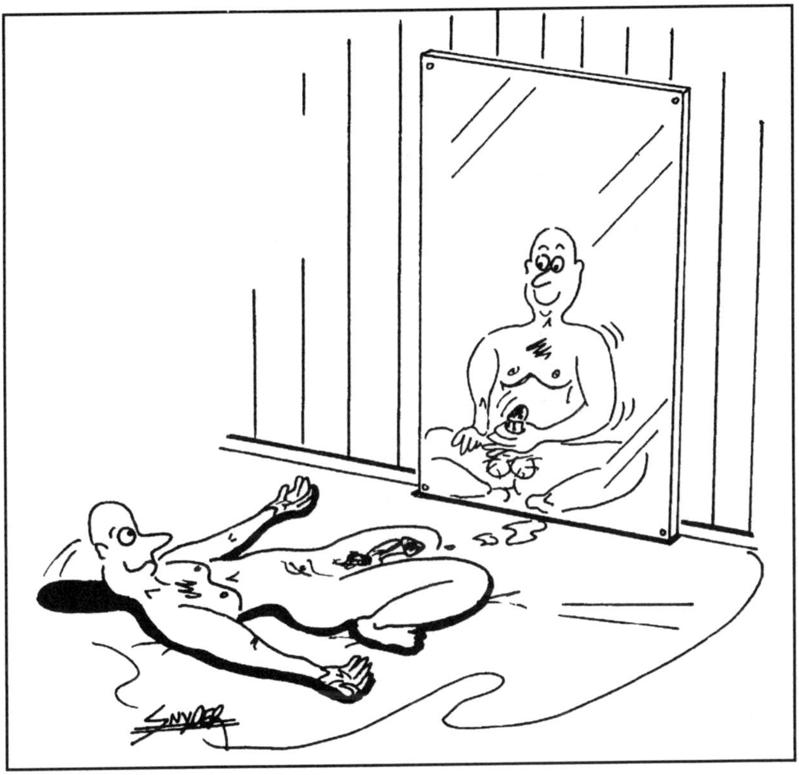
SNYDER

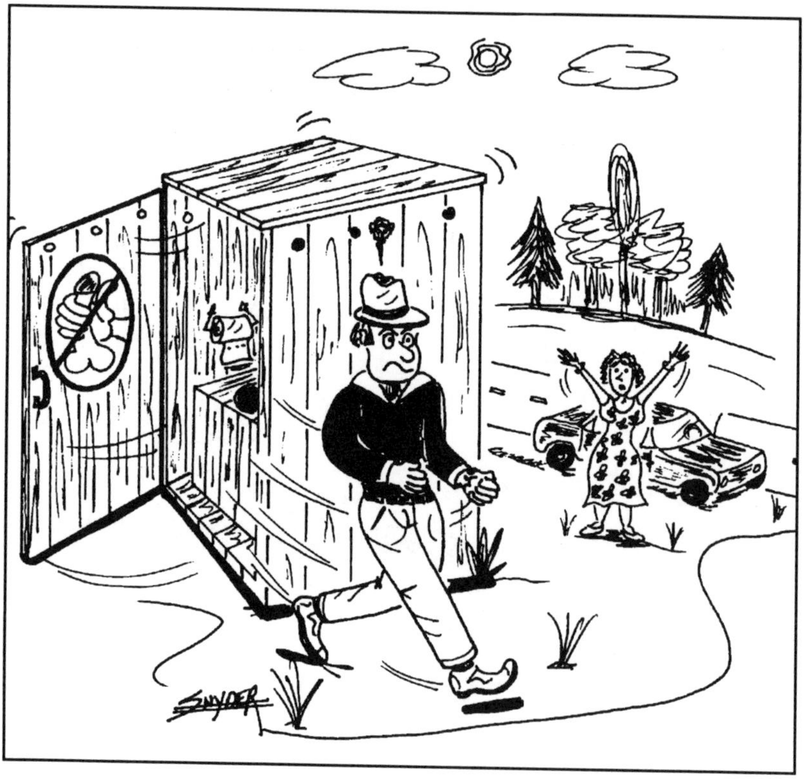
SNYDER

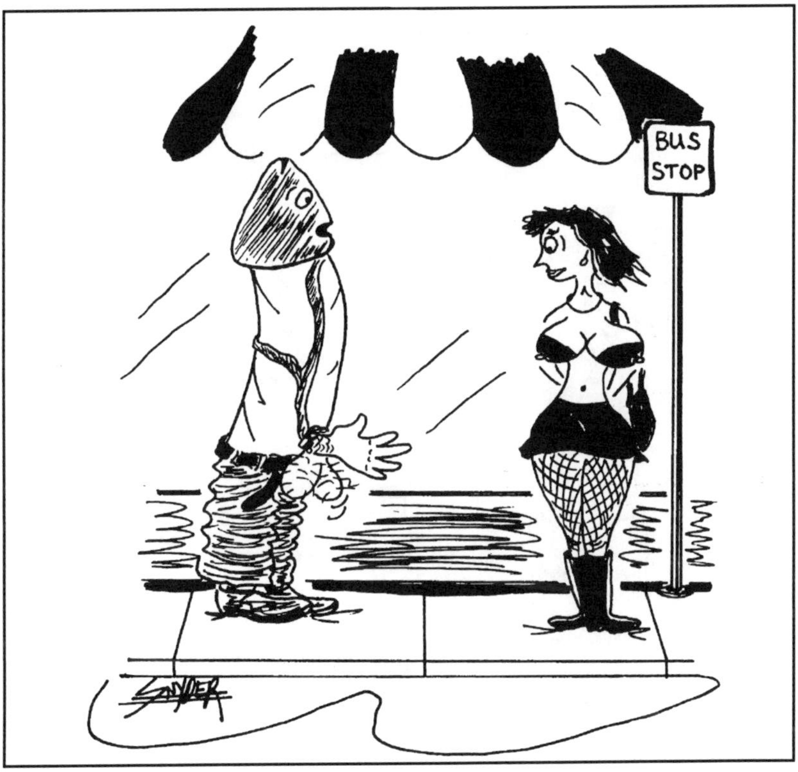
BUS
STOP

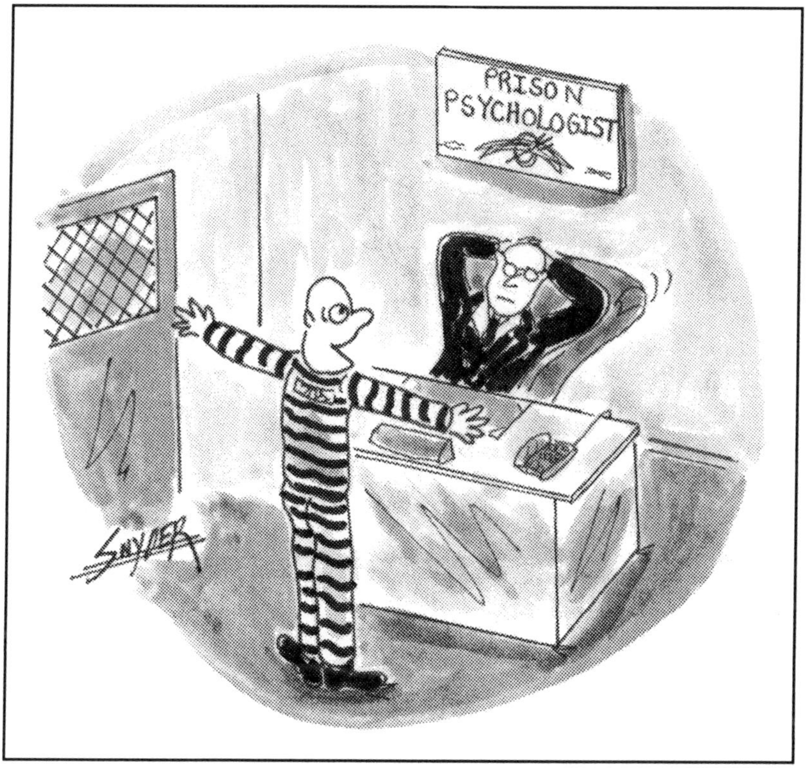
PRISON
PSYCHOLOGIST
SNYDER

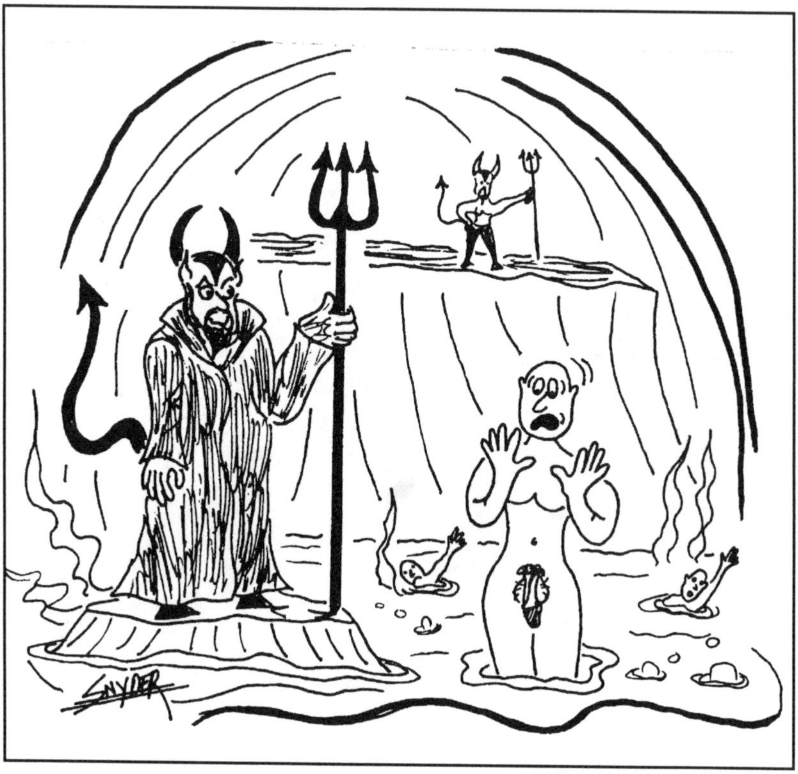
SNYDER

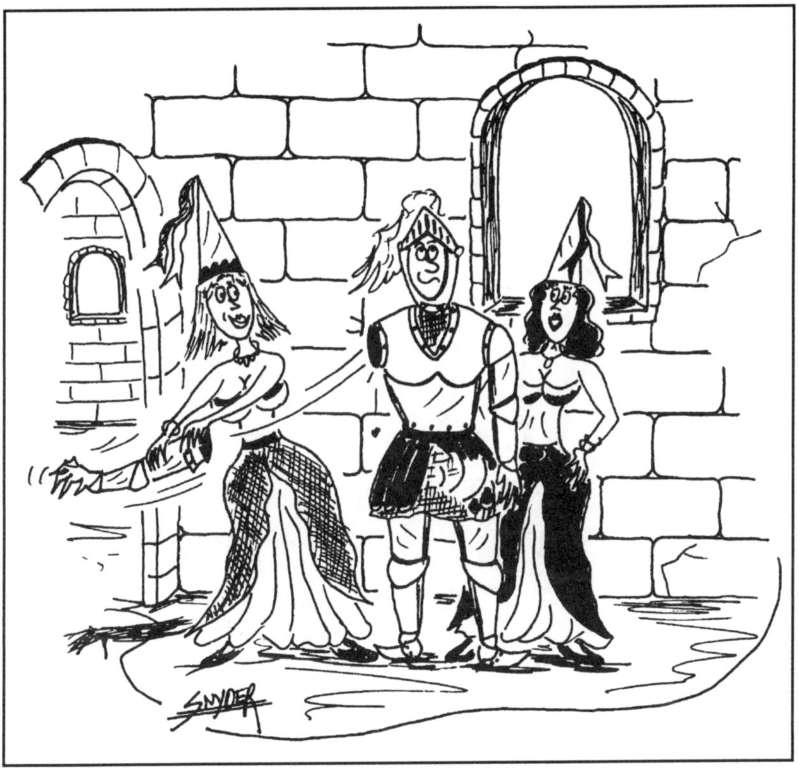
SNYDER

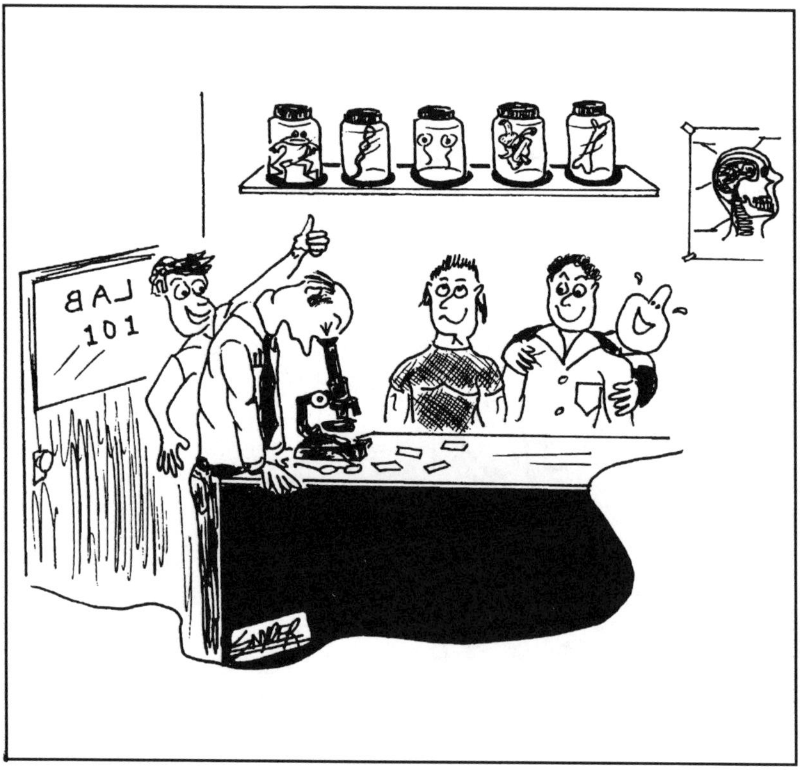
LAB
101

SNYDER

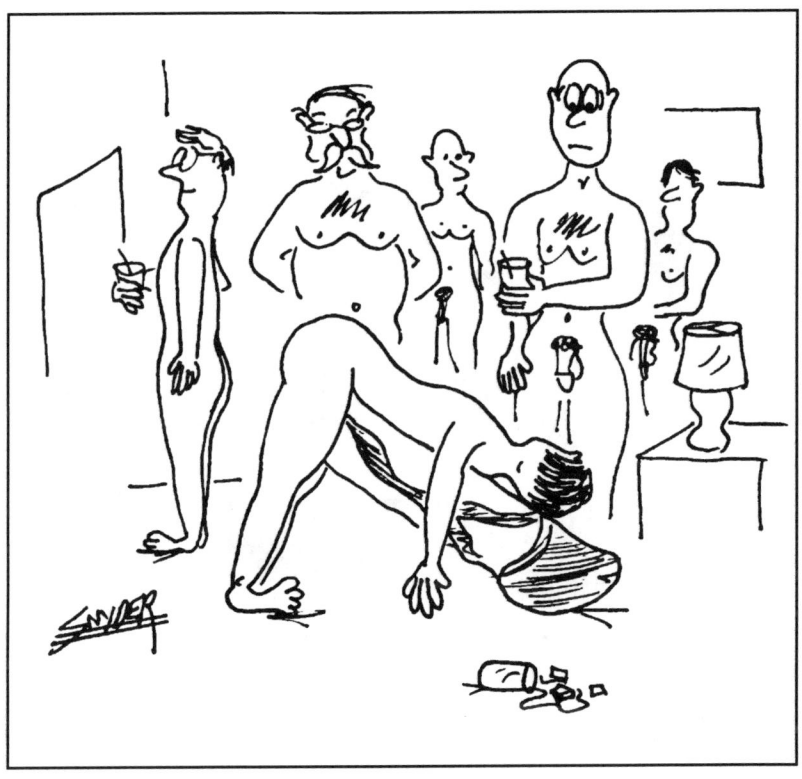

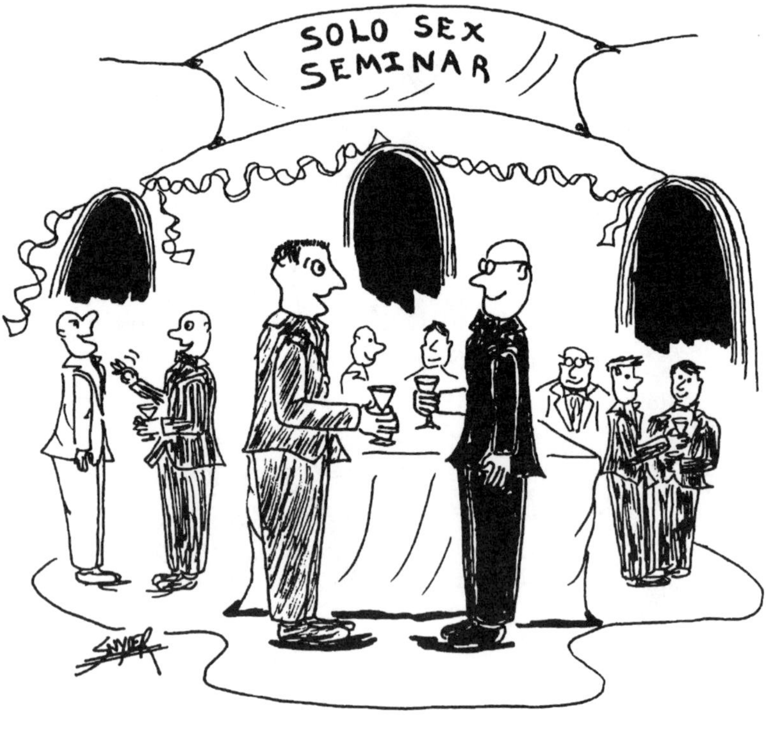
SOLO SEX
SEMINAR

CELEBRATE The Self
The Magazine of SOLO SEX
HERE'S SOME OF
WHAT YOU'VE MISSED

How to increase genital size; Solo Sex jokes; Prostate problems; Bisex; Anal masturbation; Zinc, Vitamin E.; and Sex; Japanese fertility festival; Phallic worship; Cybersex rip-off. Brinkmanship; Penile injections; Nude worship; circumcision and orgasm; Penis enlargement; Solo Sex in public; Multiple orgasms; Vacuum pumps.

Orgasm Records; Penile implants; Insertions; Full-body orgasms; Venus II evaluations; Fantasy cocks; New School for Social Masturbation. The jock as sex object; Sex and healing; Silicone balls and dick; Moon and sun rituals; Water injections; Erotic Suffocation; Naked bikers; Eunuchs; Cock and ball strap hazards; Reproducing genitals in plaster; Kinky public ations. Solosex together; Cock and ball torture; Autofellatio; Prostate pleasure; Sex behind the wheel; All time best sex; Naked in moonlight; Piercings; Sponges and cucumbers; Steel-stuffed dick.

HERE'S WHAT'S AHEAD

Readers Solo Sex Techniques,
Product Evaluations, Sex and Spirit, Art, Humor,
Cartoons, Discounts on books, videos, products.

Editorial coverage in *Playboy, Men's Health, Gallery, Men's Confidential, Factsheet Five,* and *Sex: A Man's Guide* (Rodale).

"There's no better publication on male sexuality on the market today, and its consistently helpful, positive, healthy tone and holistic viewpoint are welcome counters to the sex-negative, guilt-ridden, and insidiously destructive propaganda of the fundamentalists."—James H., MA

( ) CTS (1 yr 6 issues) $24.95
Canada, Mexico add $4.00 p&h; other
countries add $15.00
( ) CTS (2 yrs) $39.95

FACTOR PRESS, Dept JB
P.O. Box 8888
Mobile, AL 36689
MC/VISA call 1-800-304-0077
Or write for information.